I0467616

The Complete Guide To Drawing Pokemon Volume 10

Pokemon Drawing for Beginners: Full Guide Volume 10

How to Draw Pokemon

By : Gala Publication

2

Published By :

Gala Publication
© Copyright 2015 – Gala Publication

ISBN-13: **978-1522801658**
ISBN-10: **1522801650**

Table of Contents

4

BRELOOM

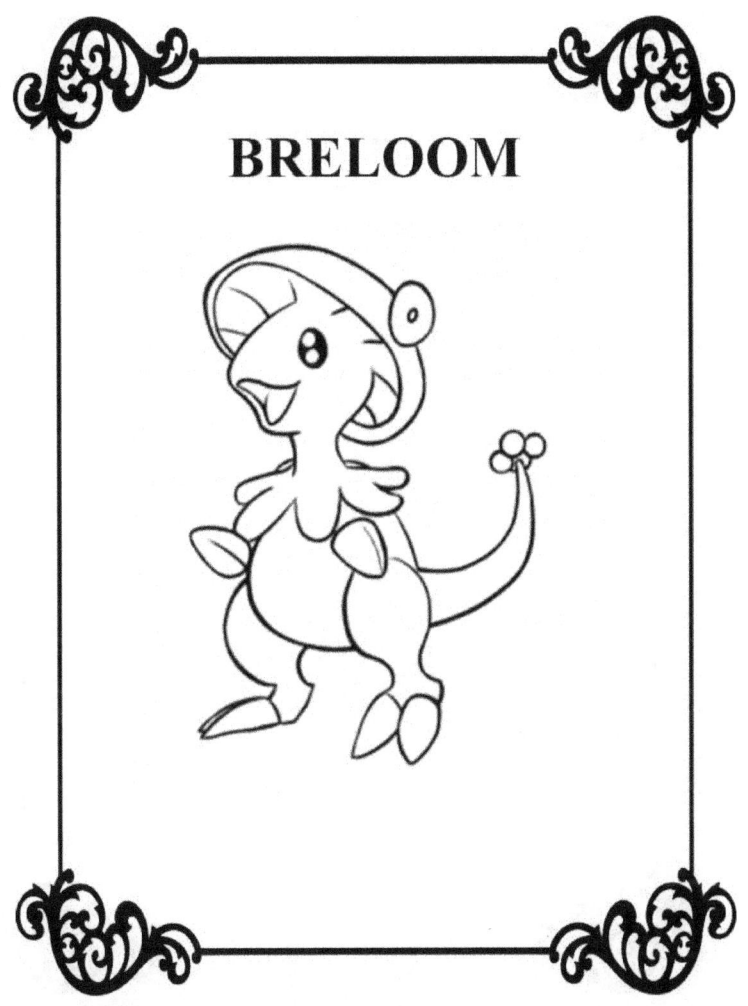

STEP 1

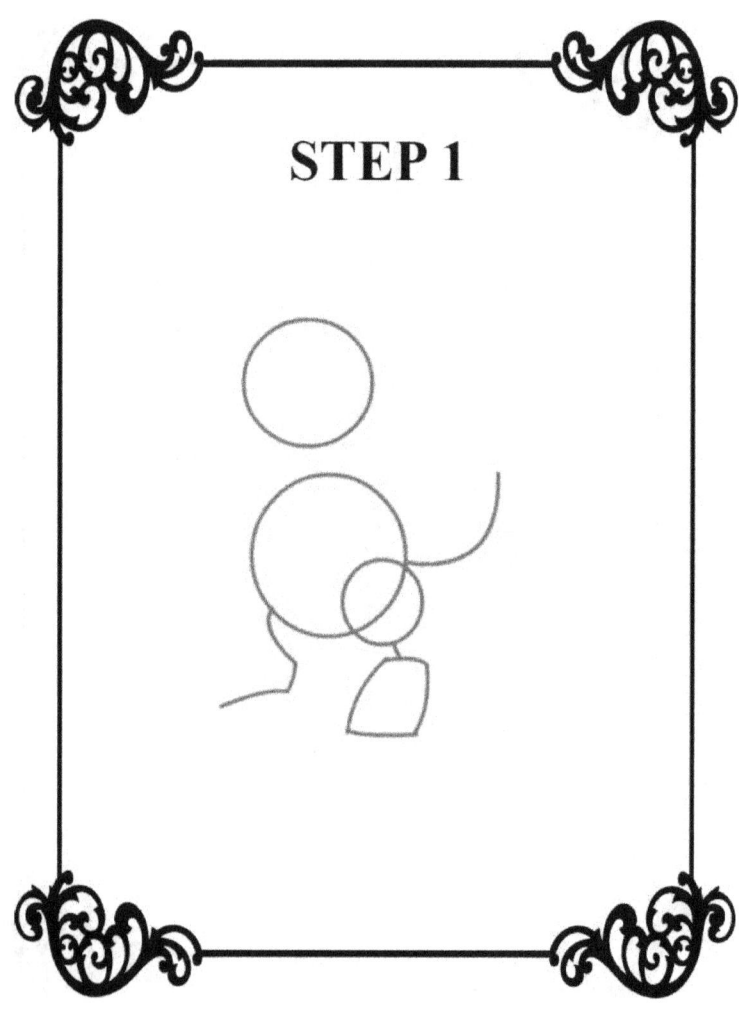

7

STEP 2

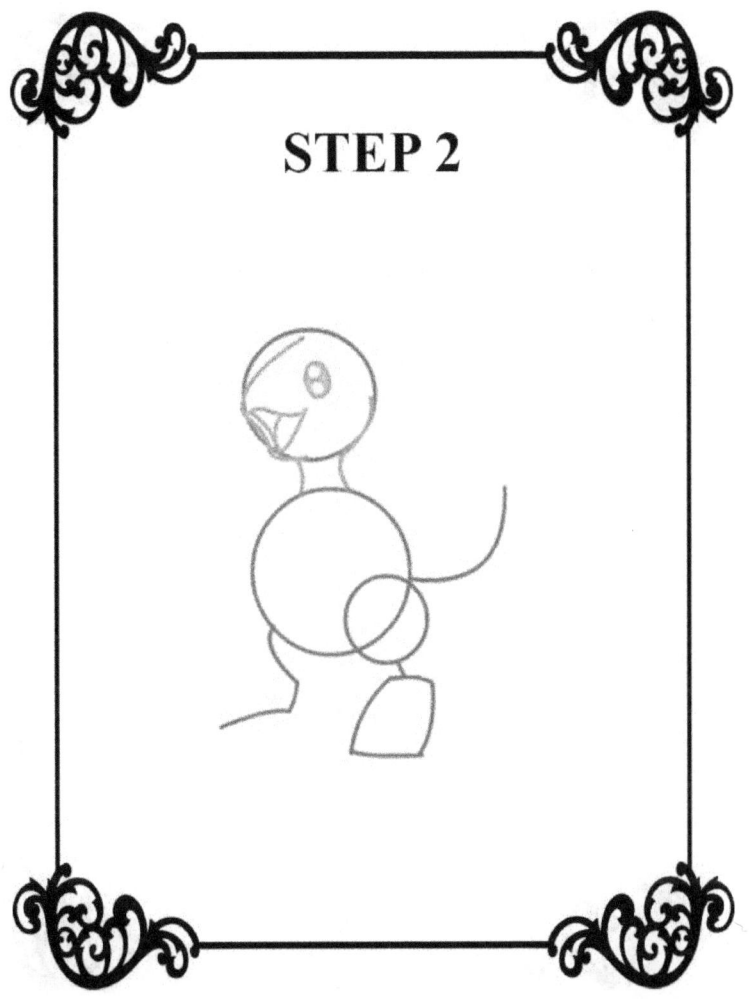

STEP 3

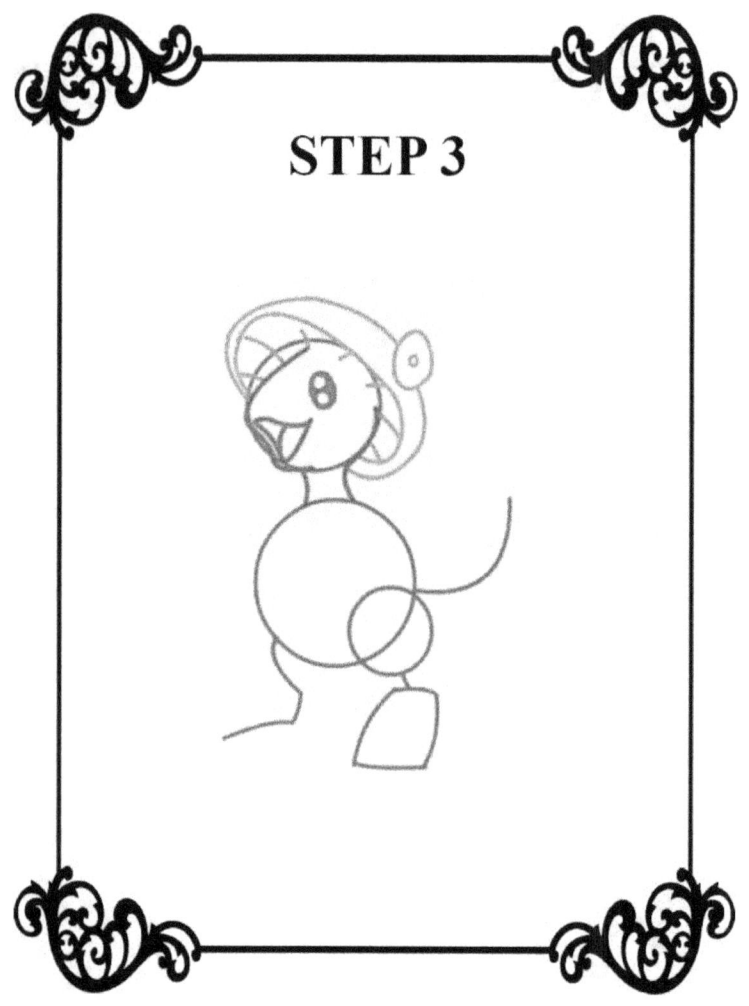

STEP 4

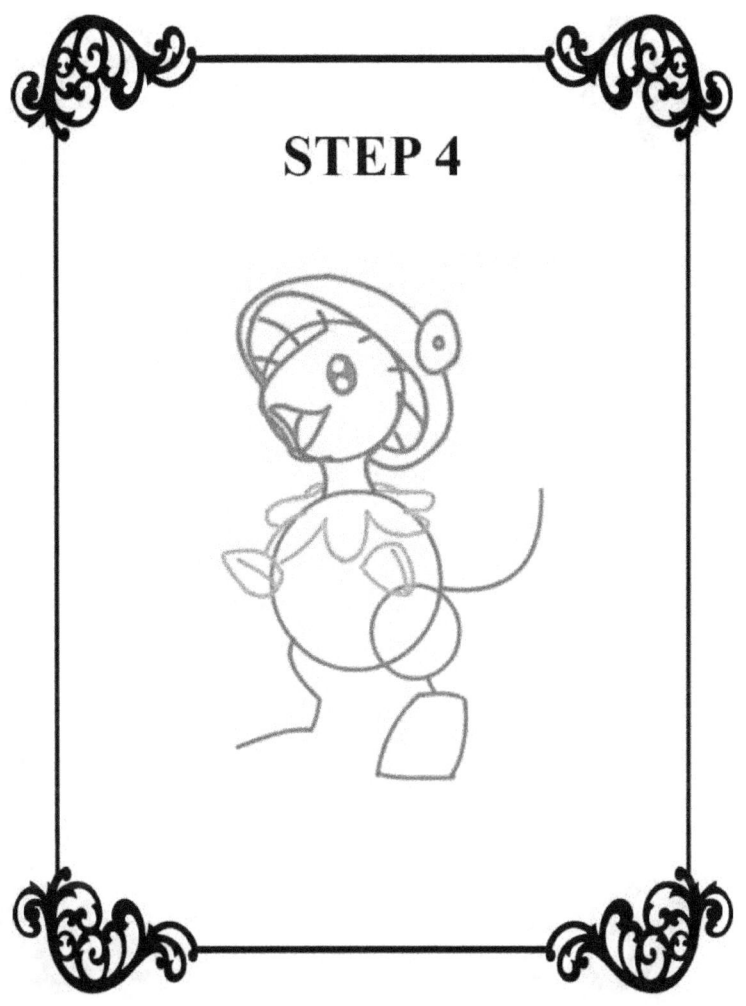

STEP 5

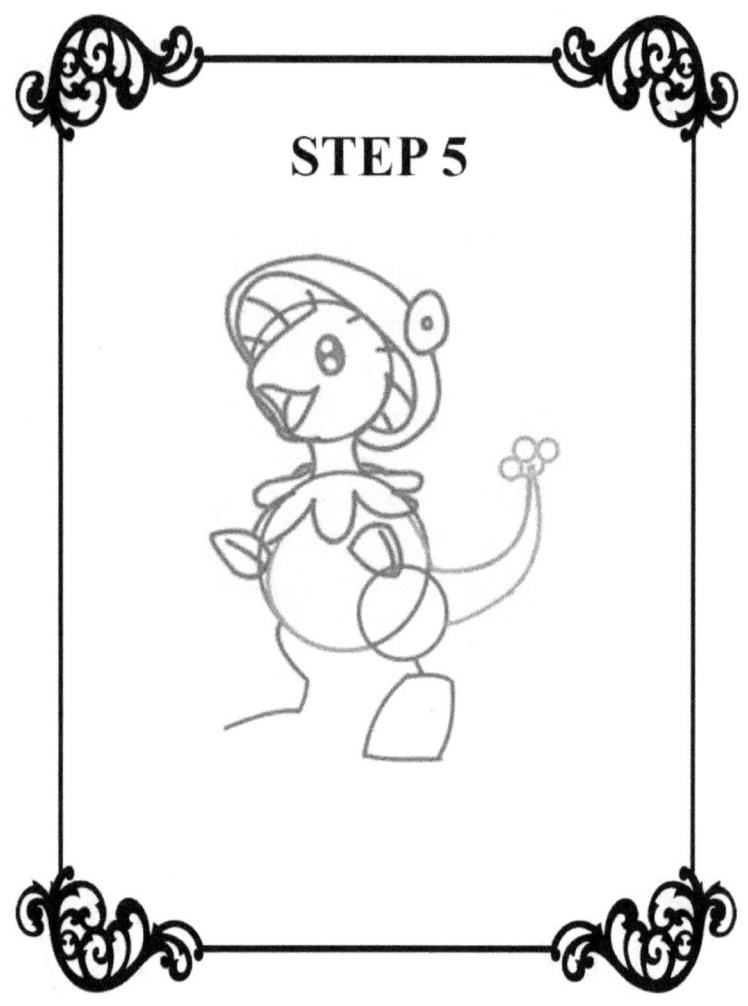

STEP 6

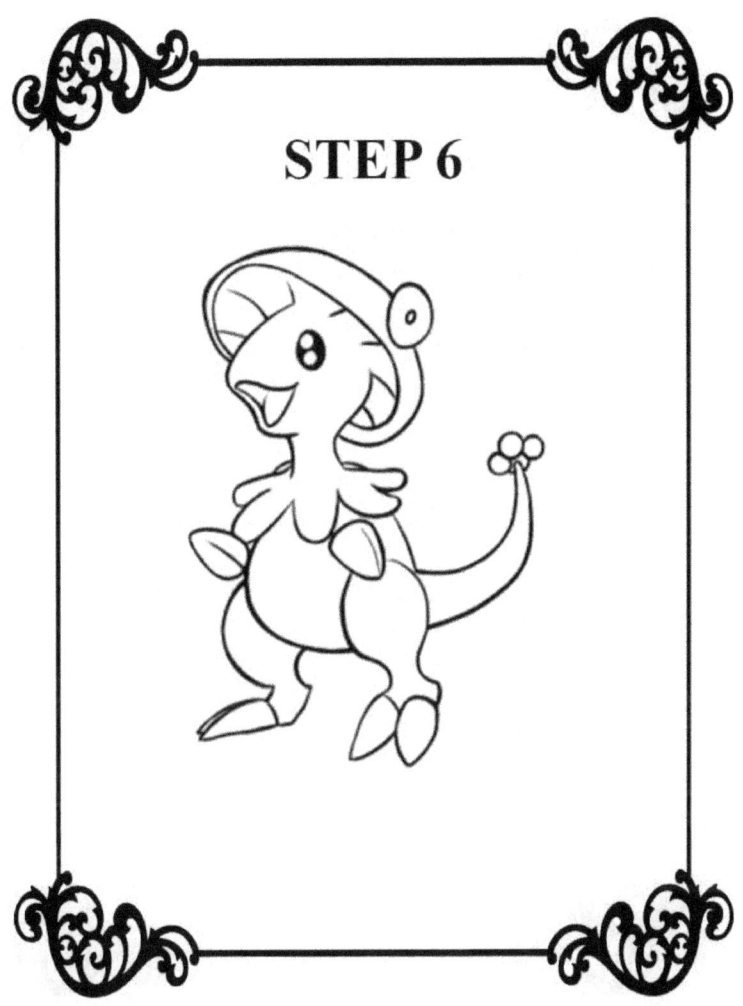

CHARMANDER

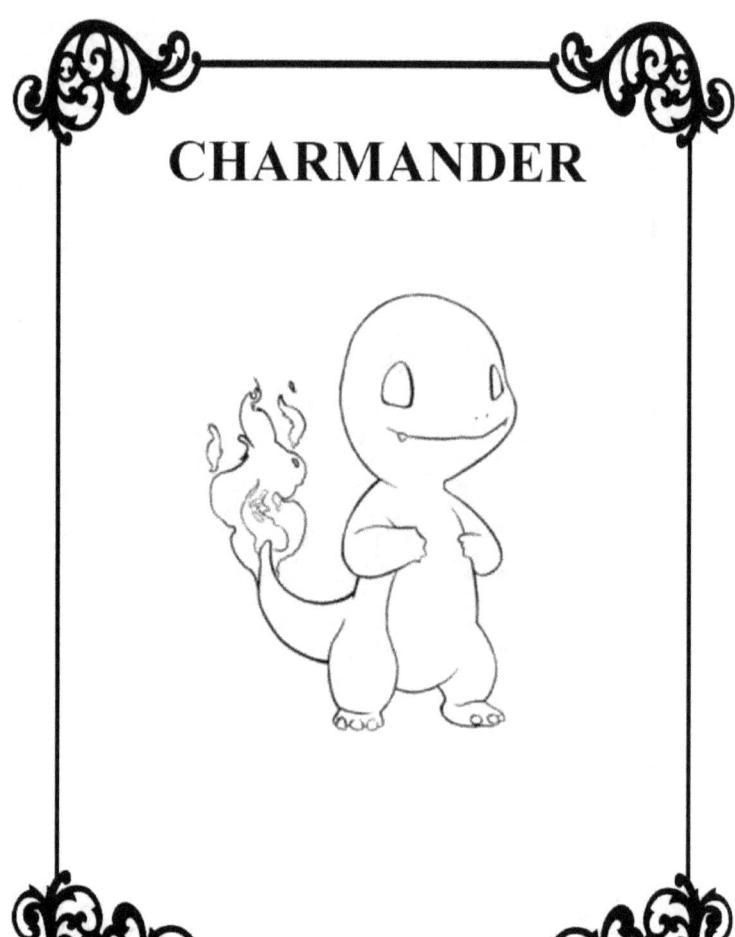

STEP 1

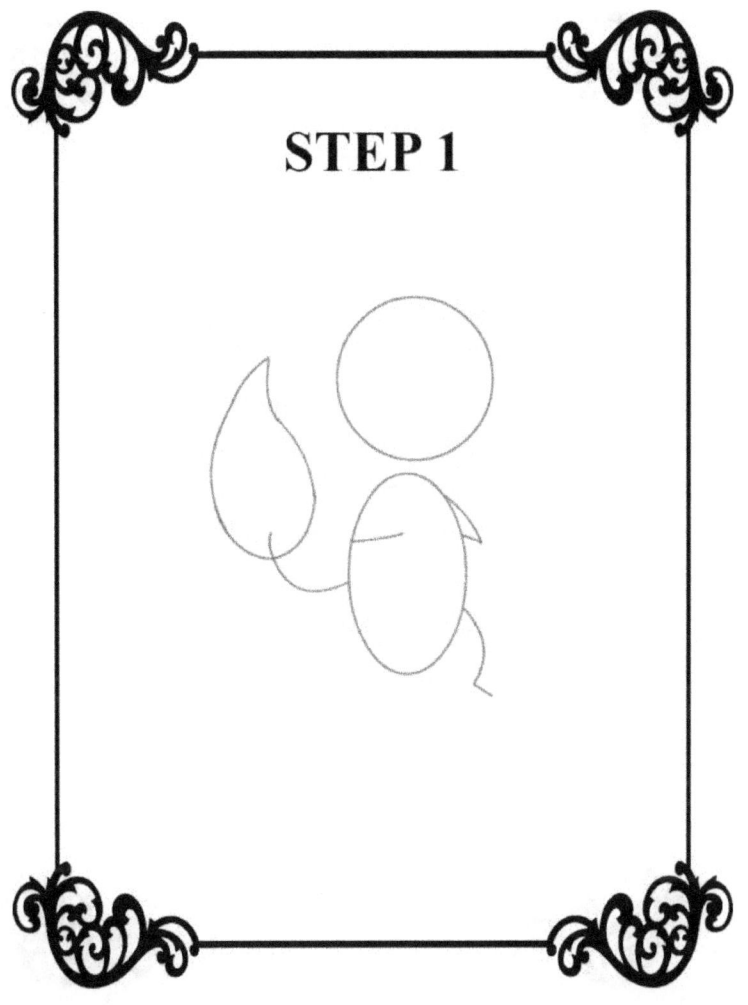

STEP 2

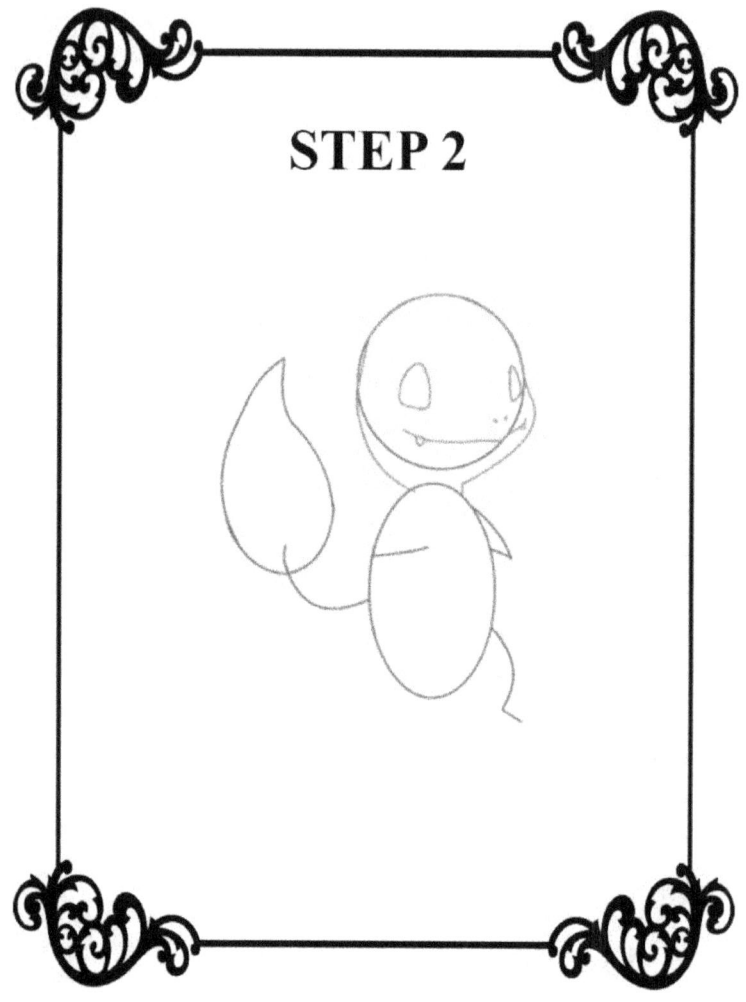

STEP 3

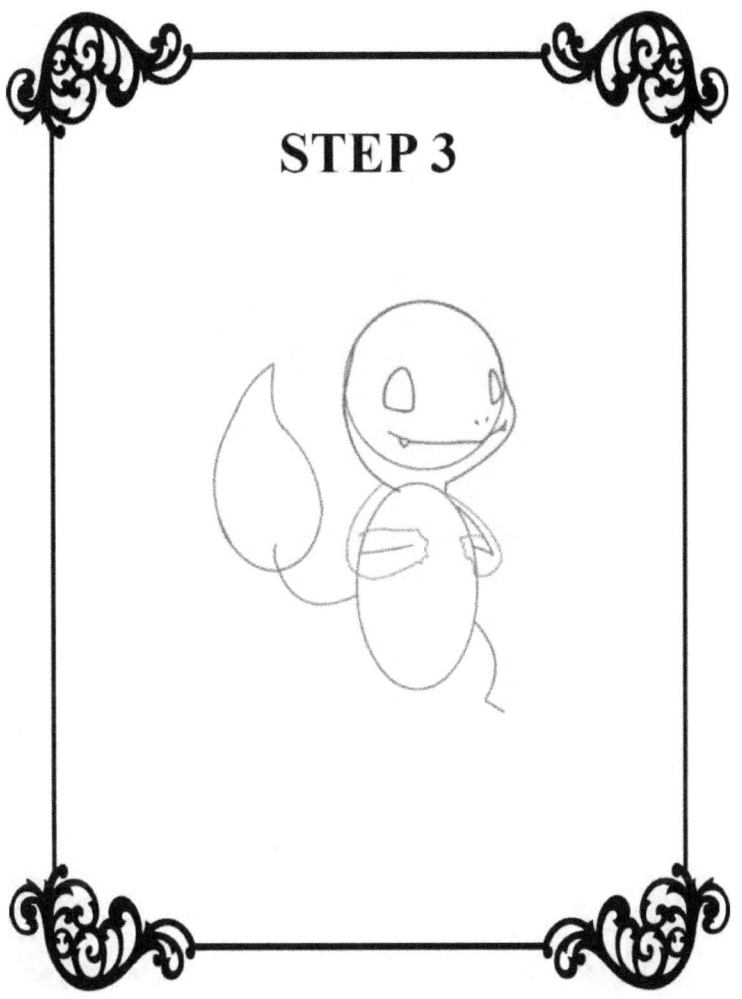

STEP 4

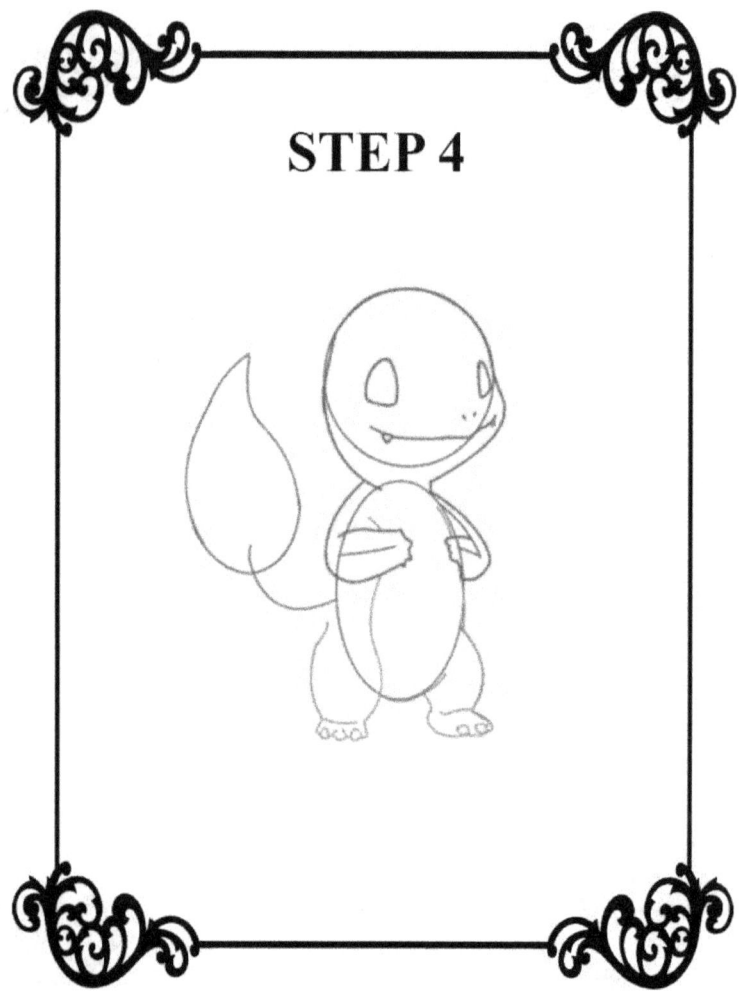

STEP 5

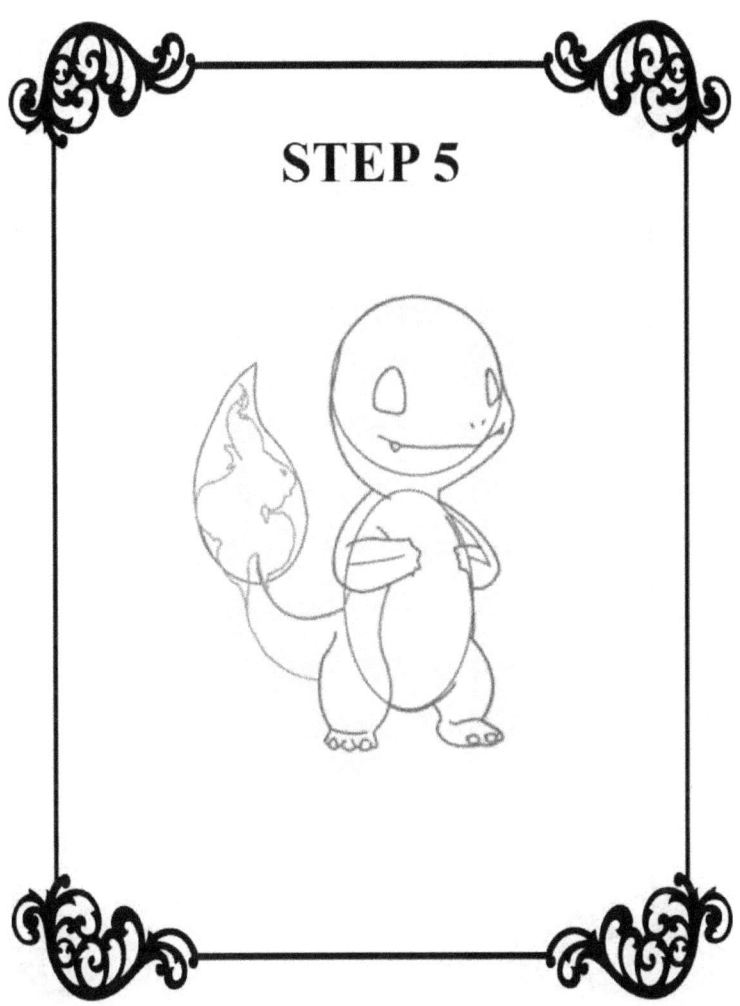

STEP 6

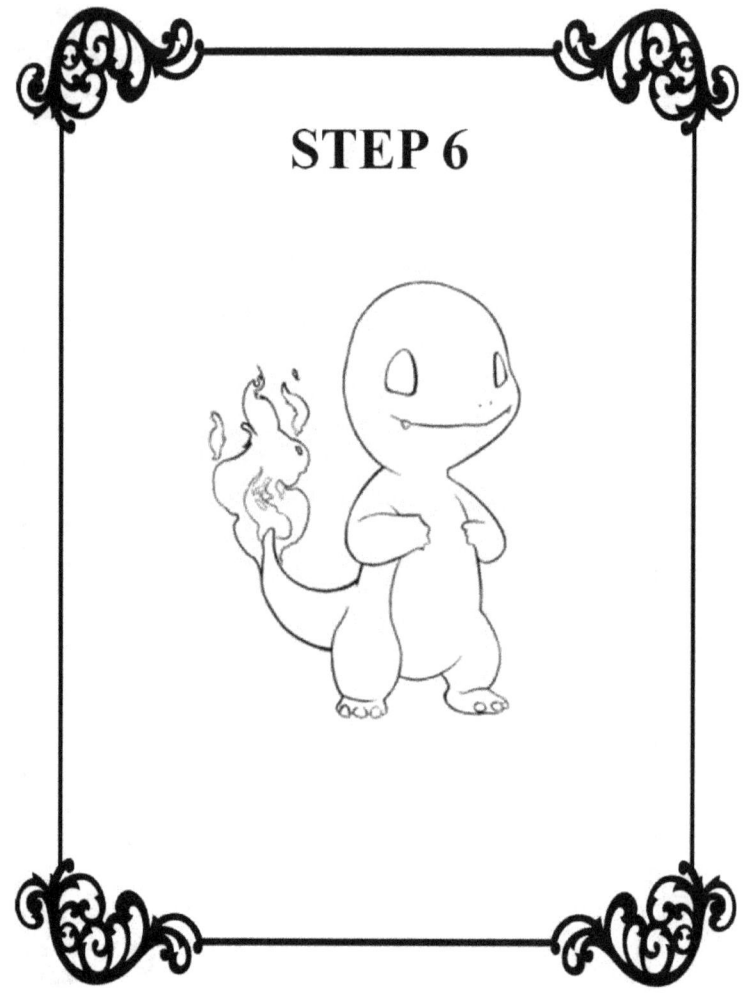

DRATINI

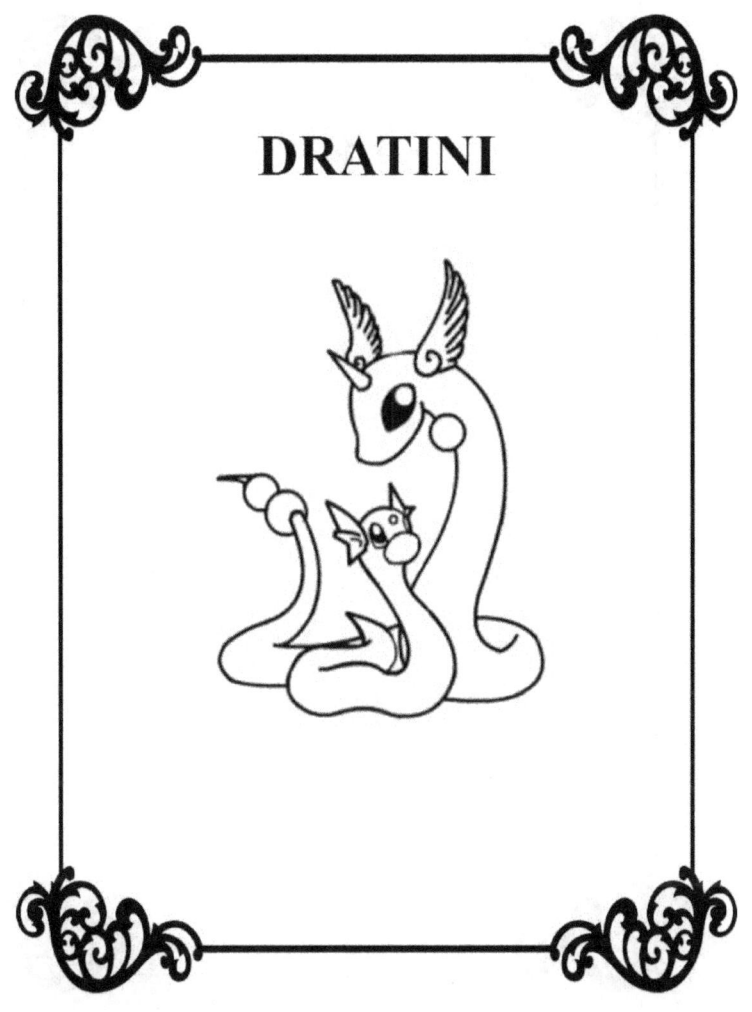

STEP 1

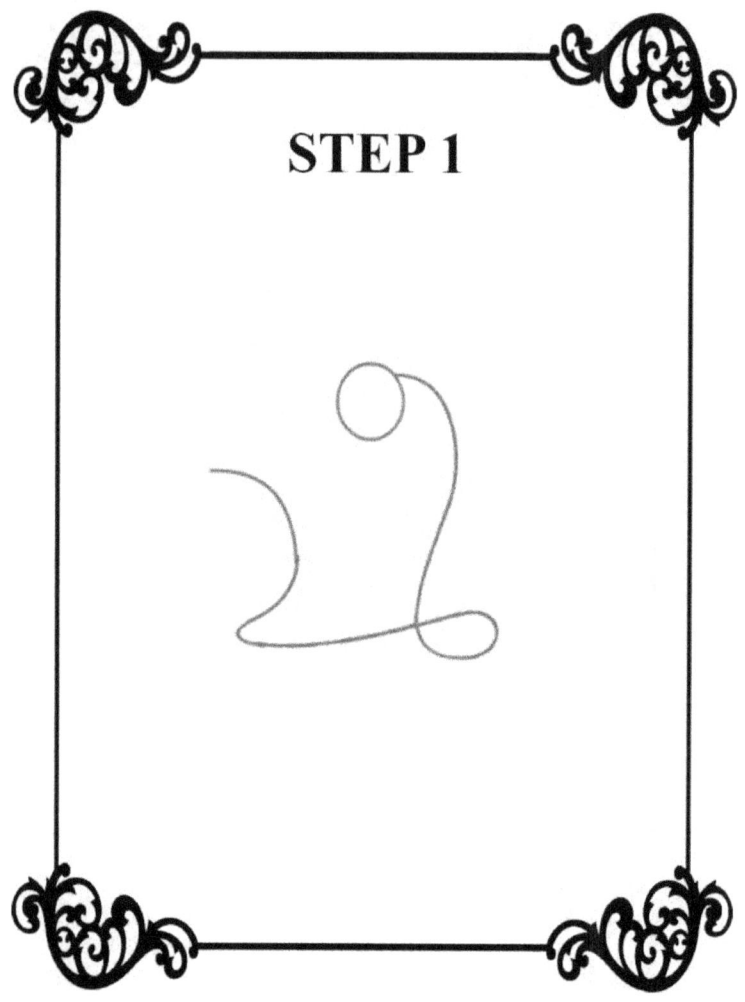

STEP 2

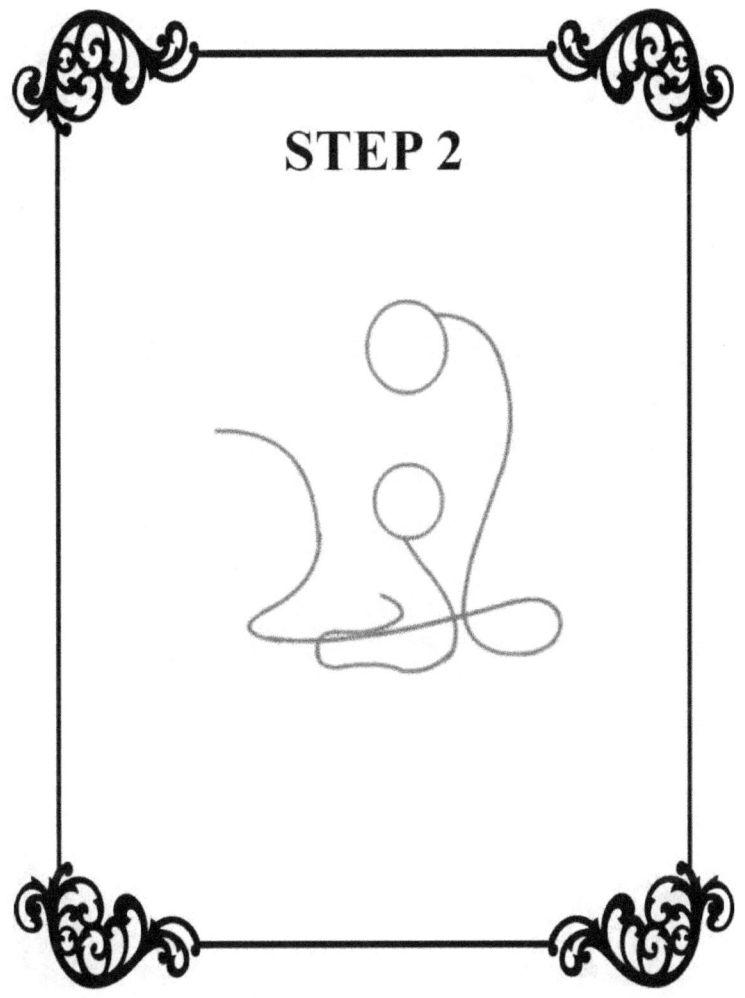

STEP 3

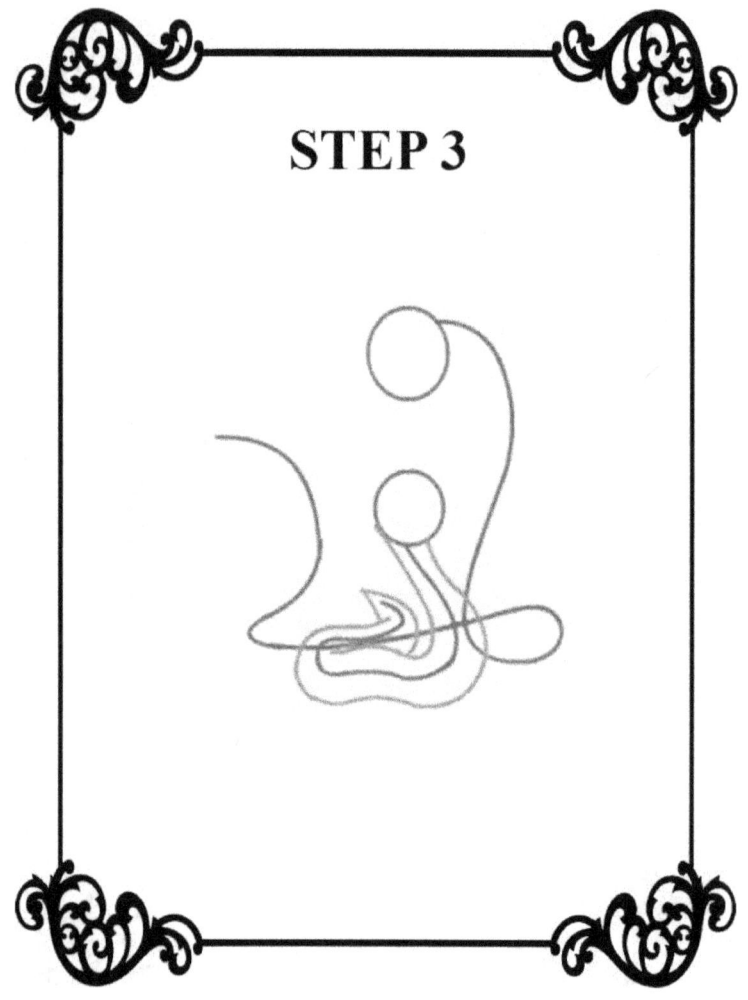

STEP 4

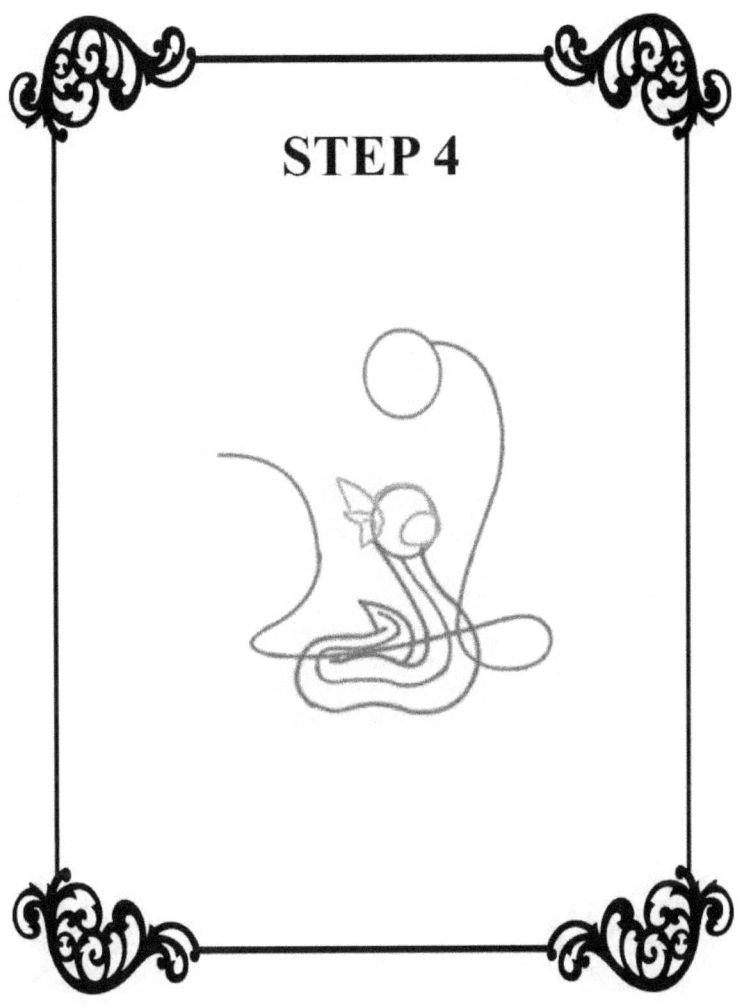

STEP 5

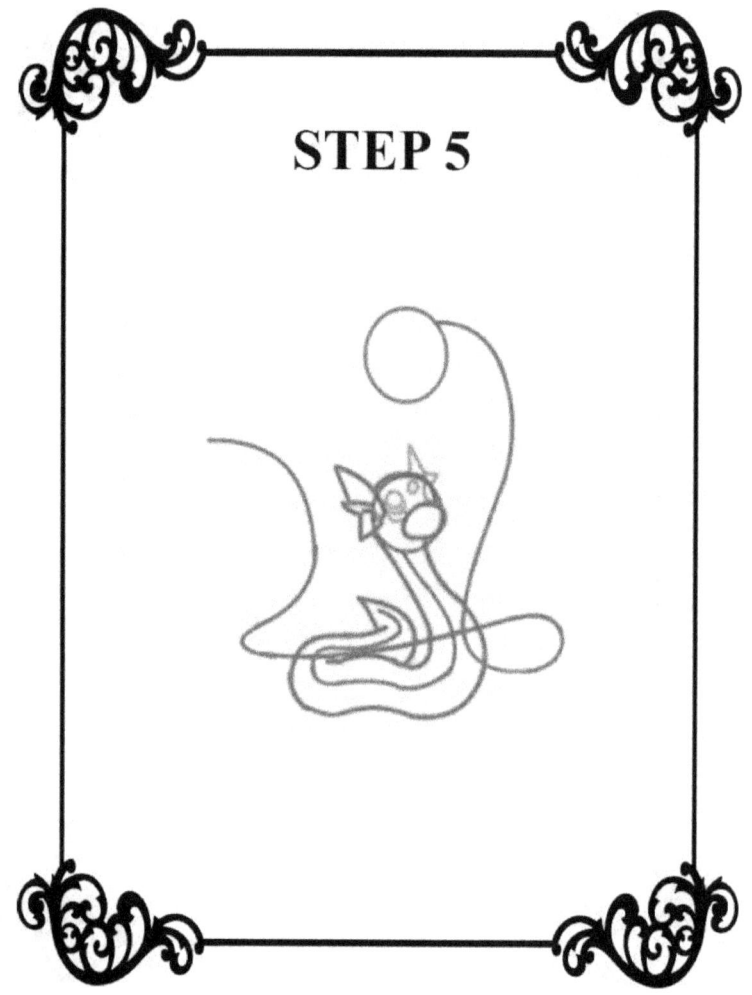

STEP 6

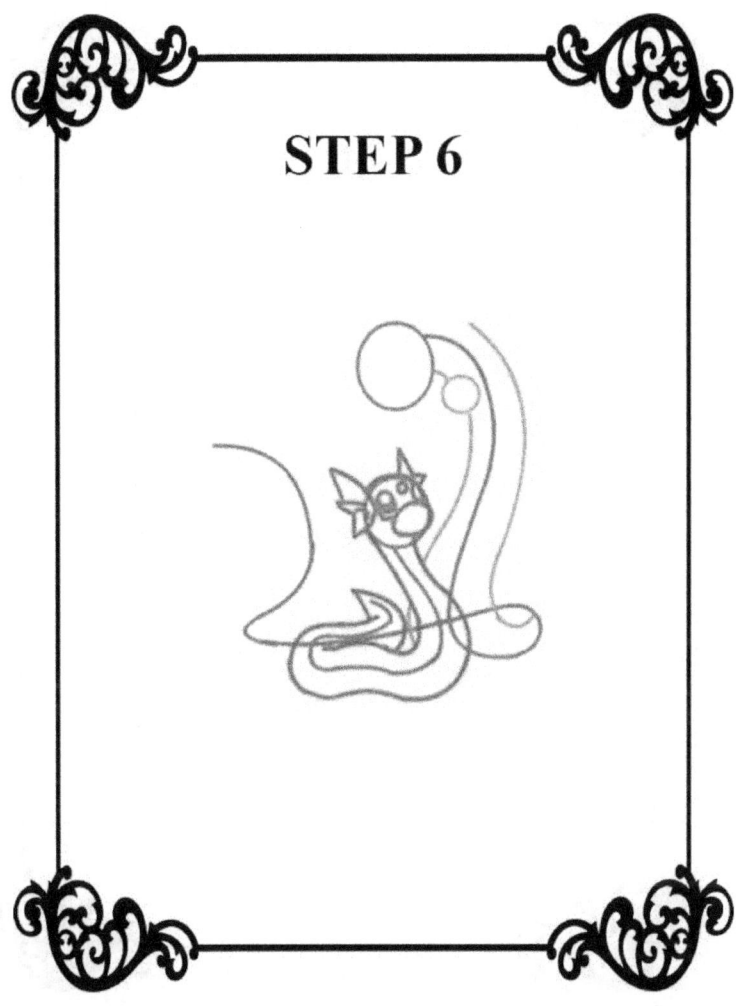

STEP 7

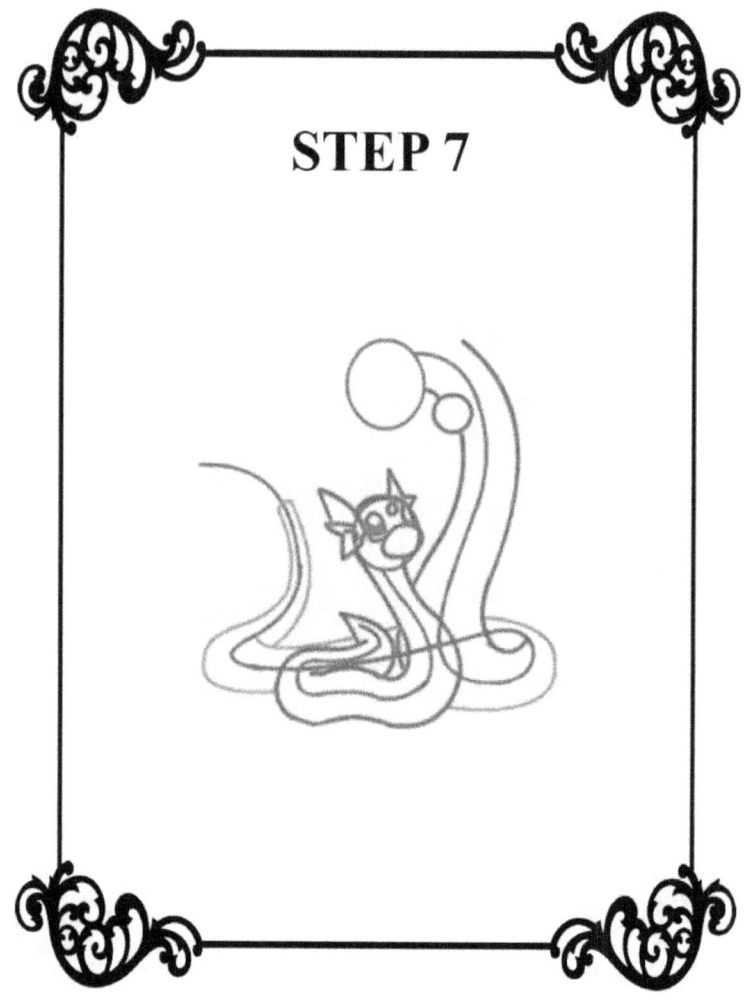

STEP 8

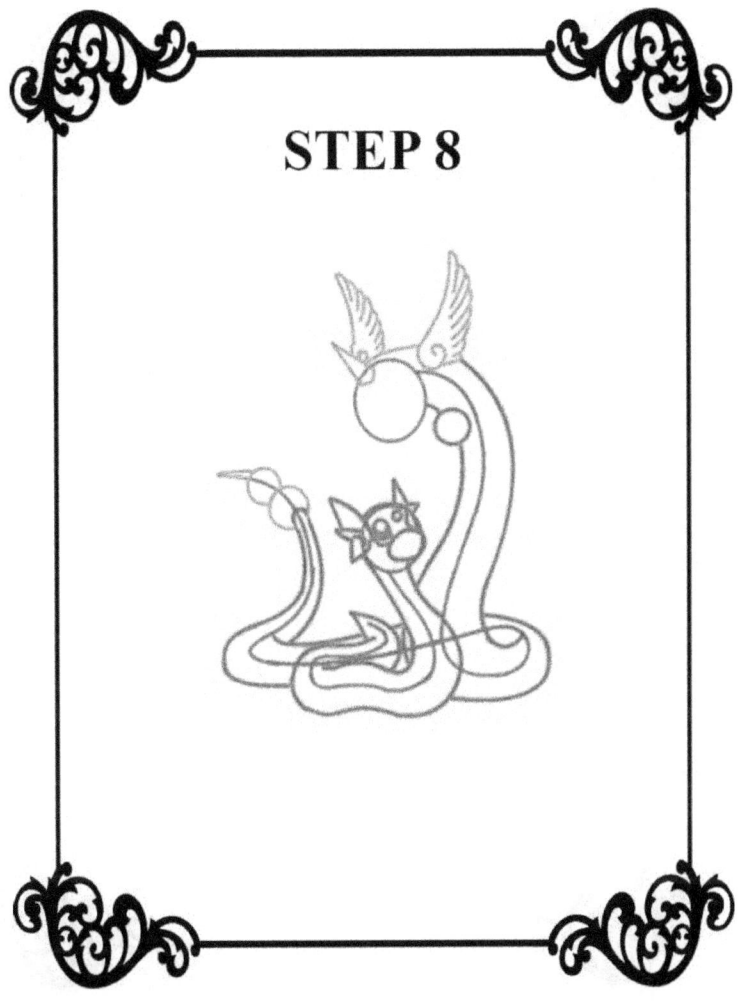

STEP 9

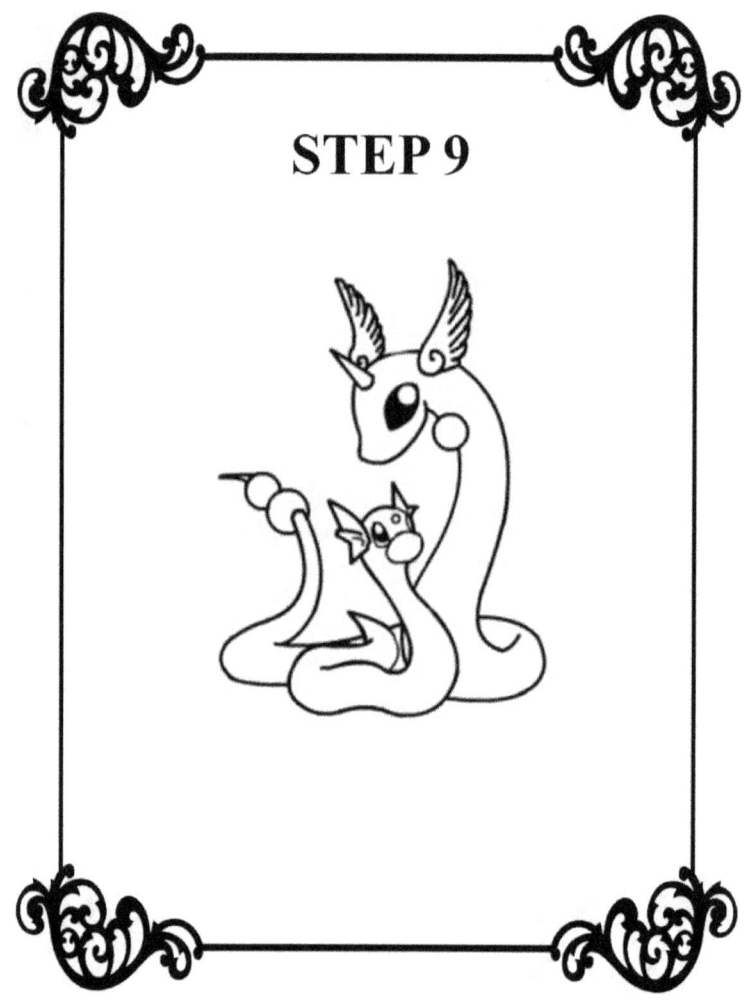

KELDEO

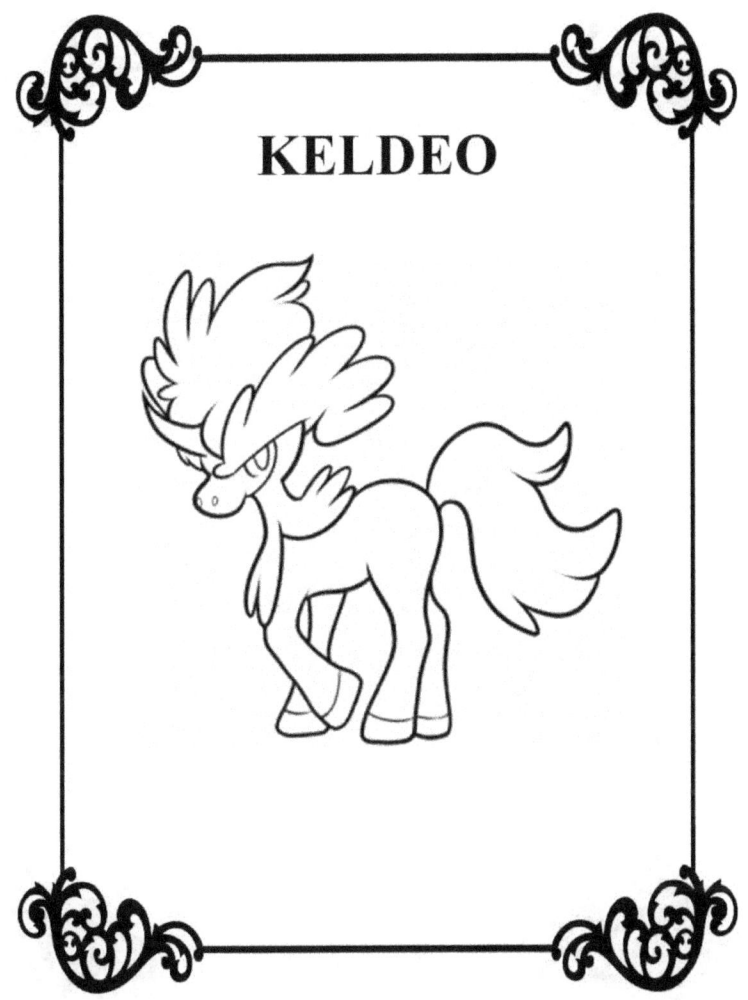

STEP 1

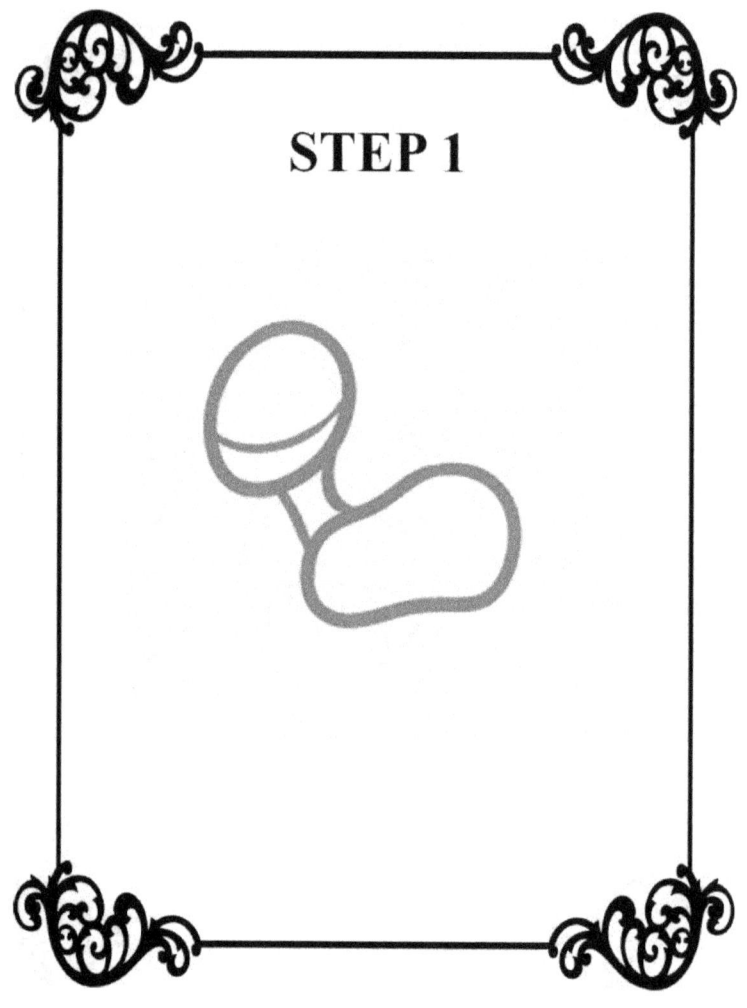

STEP 2

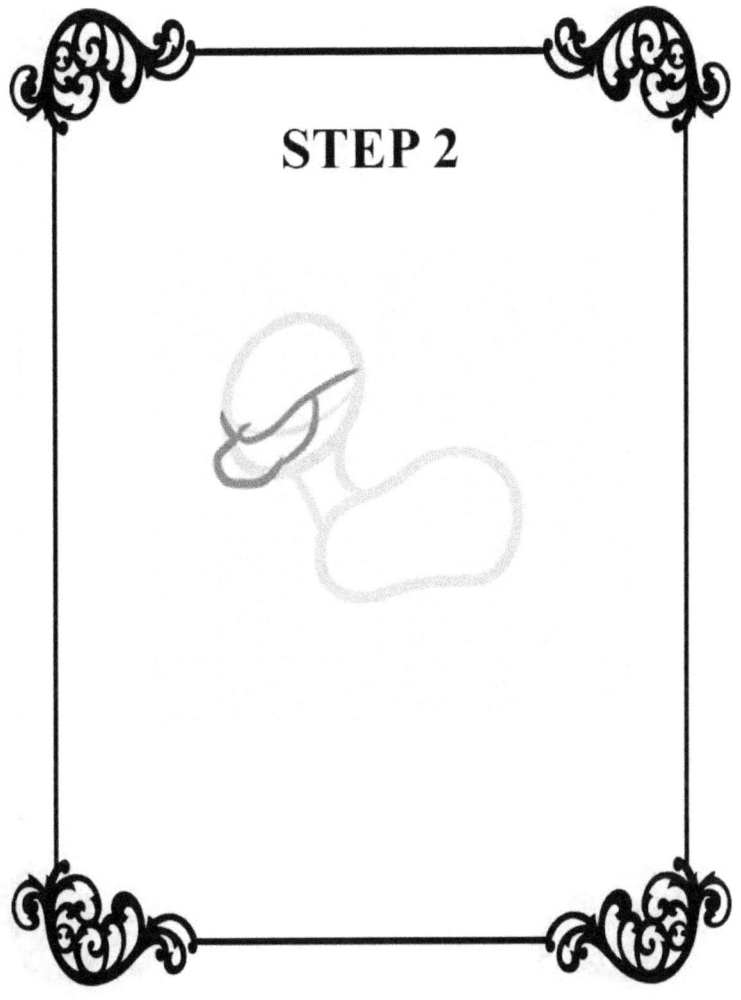

STEP 3

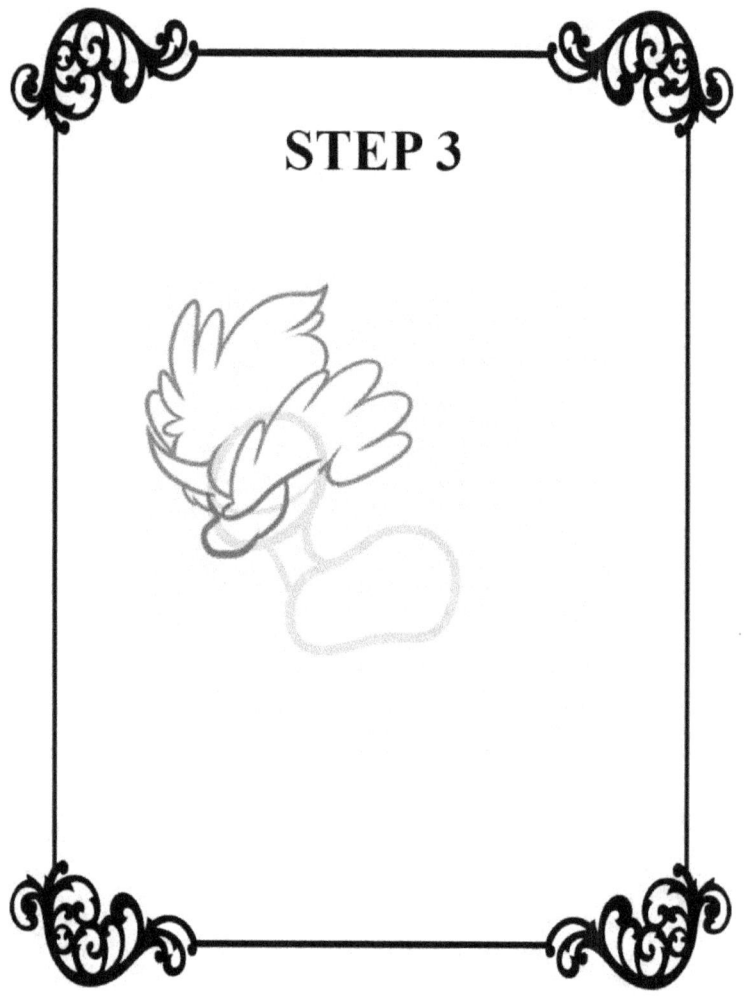

STEP 4

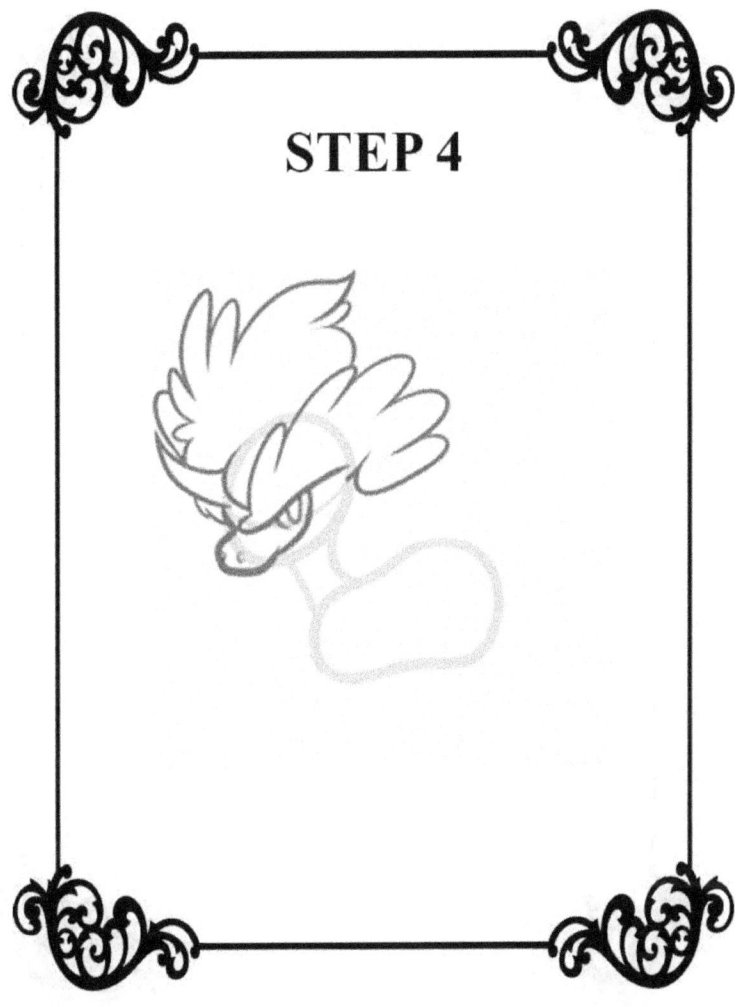

STEP 5

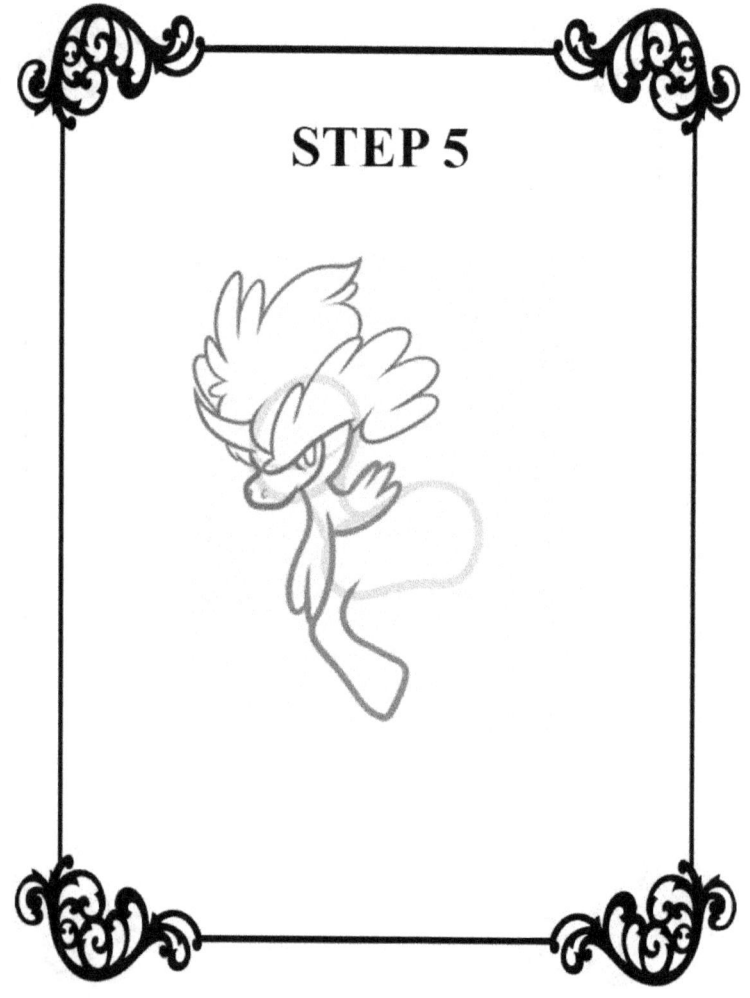

STEP 6

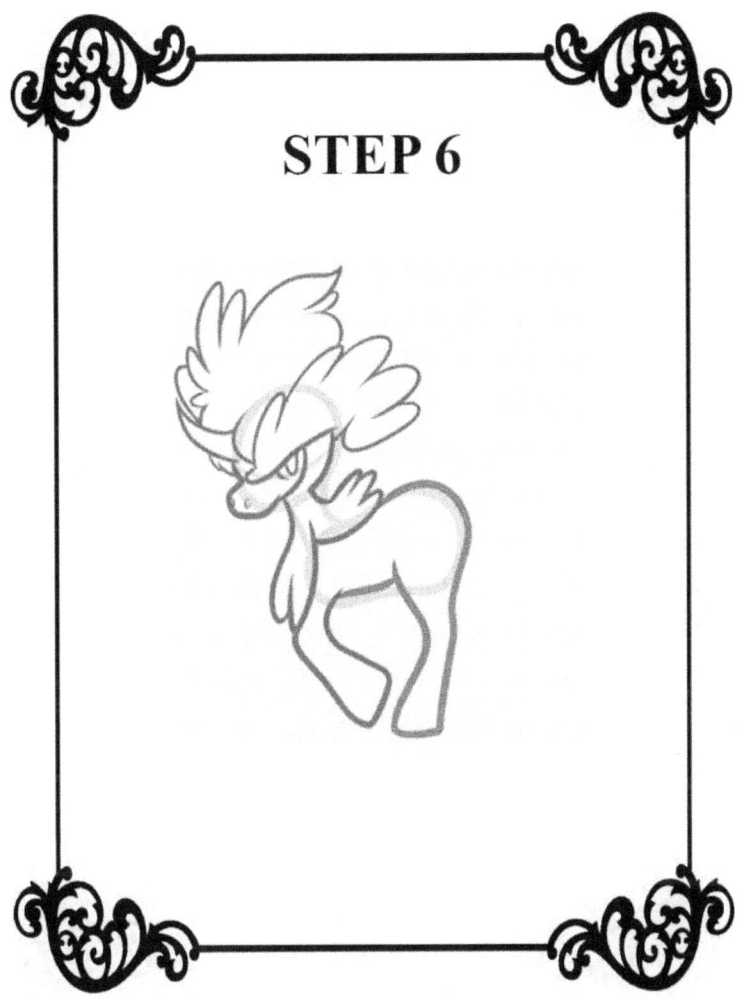

STEP 7

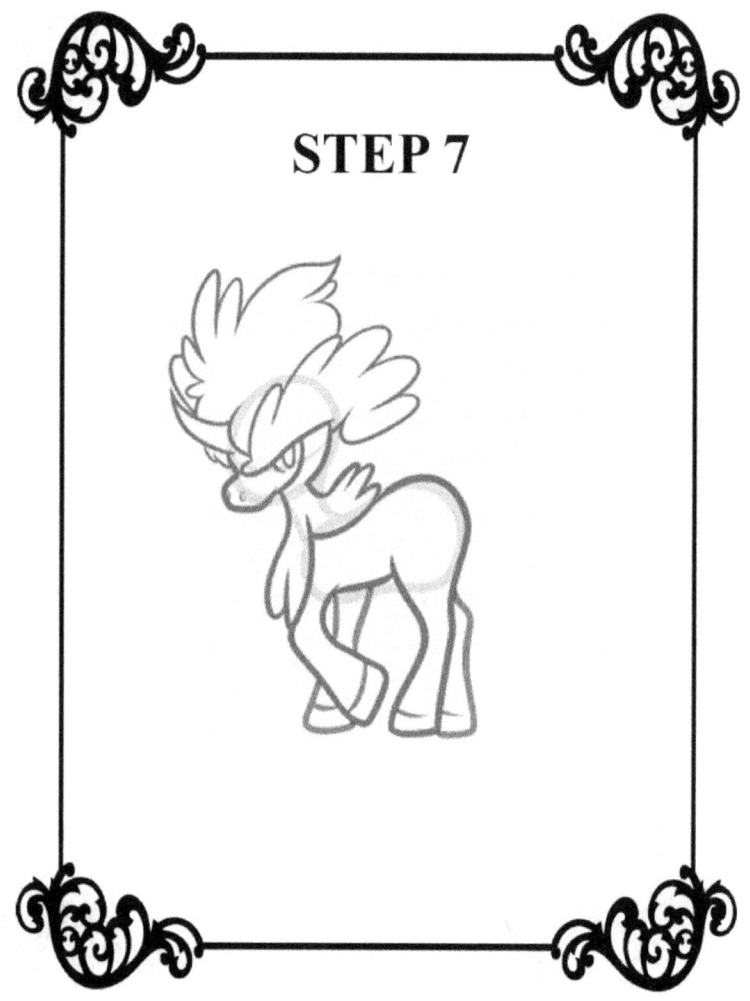

STEP 8

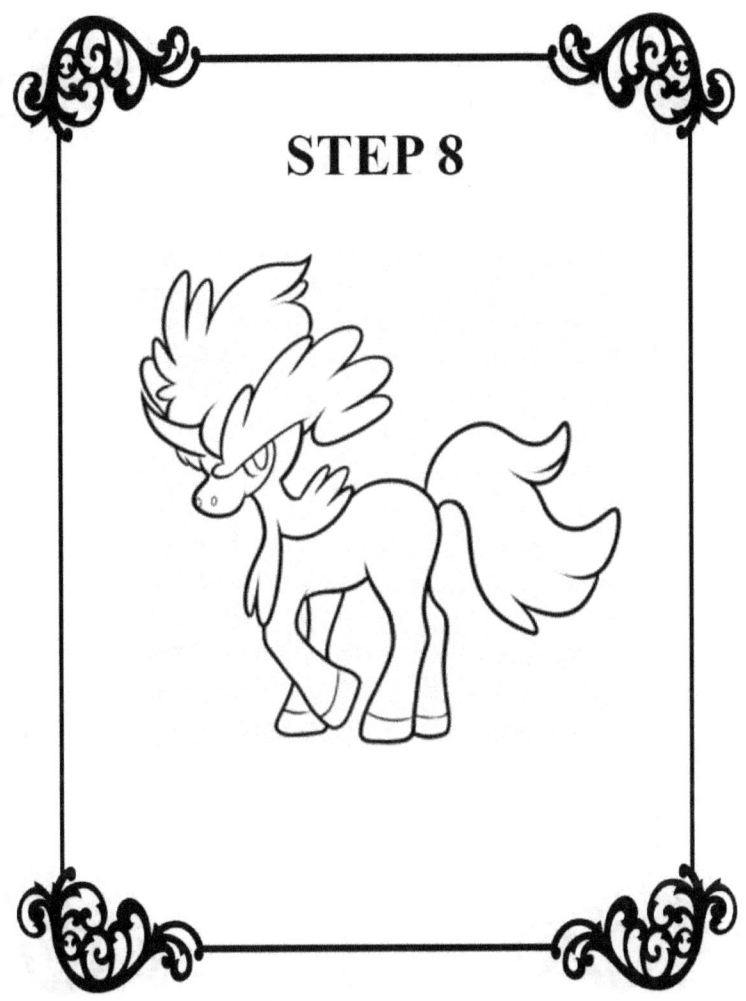

LAPRAS

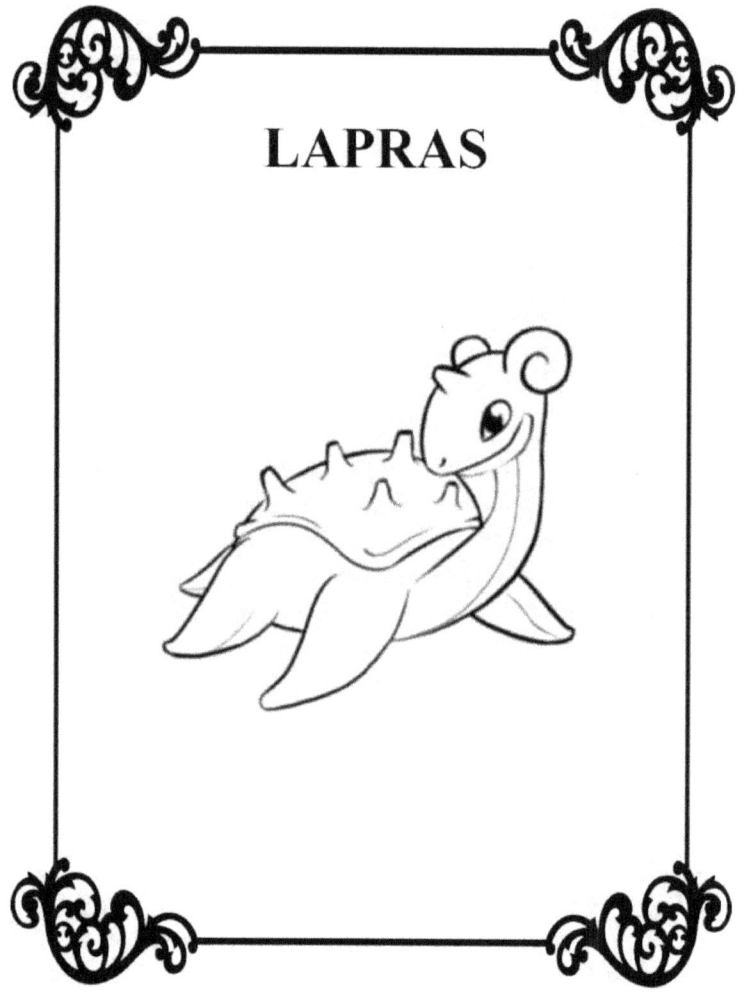

STEP 1

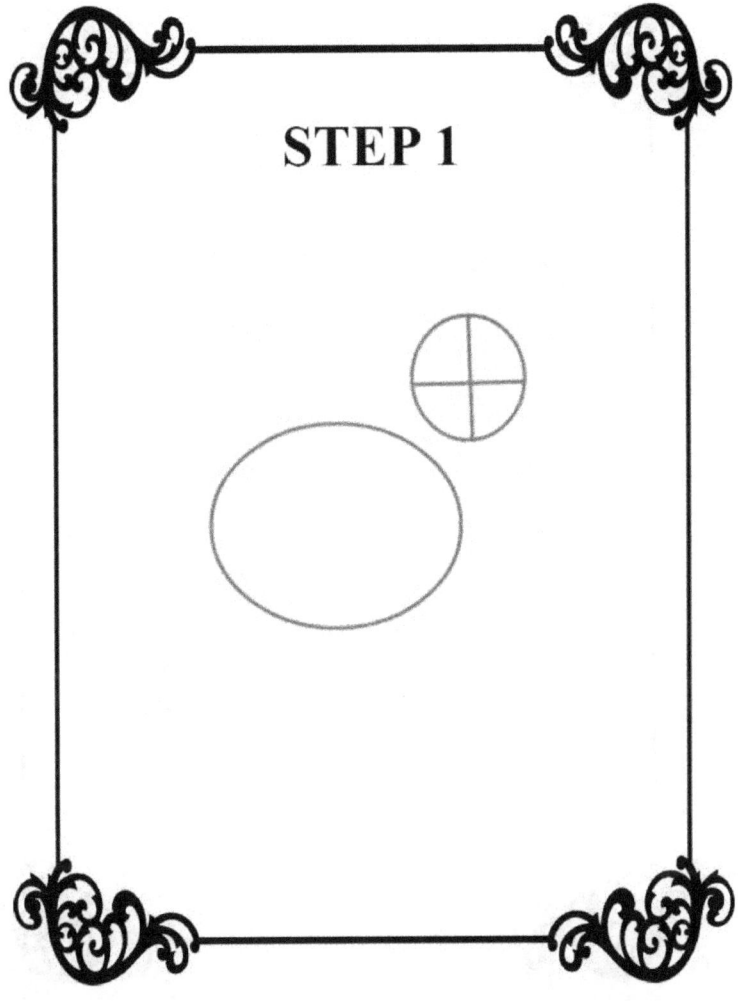

STEP 2

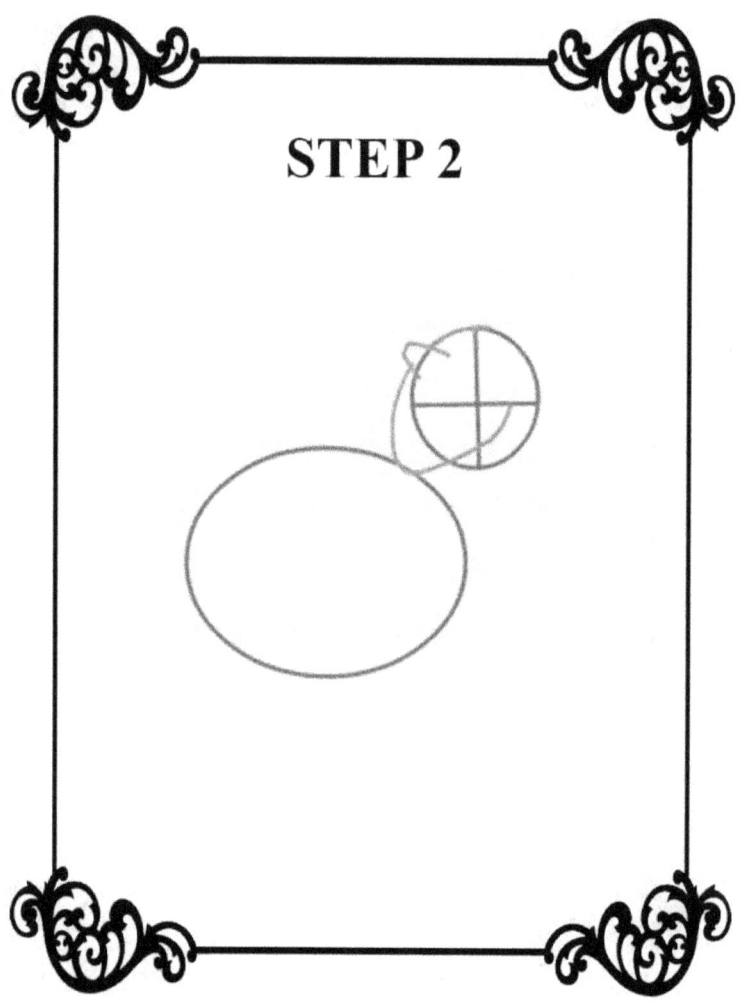

STEP 3

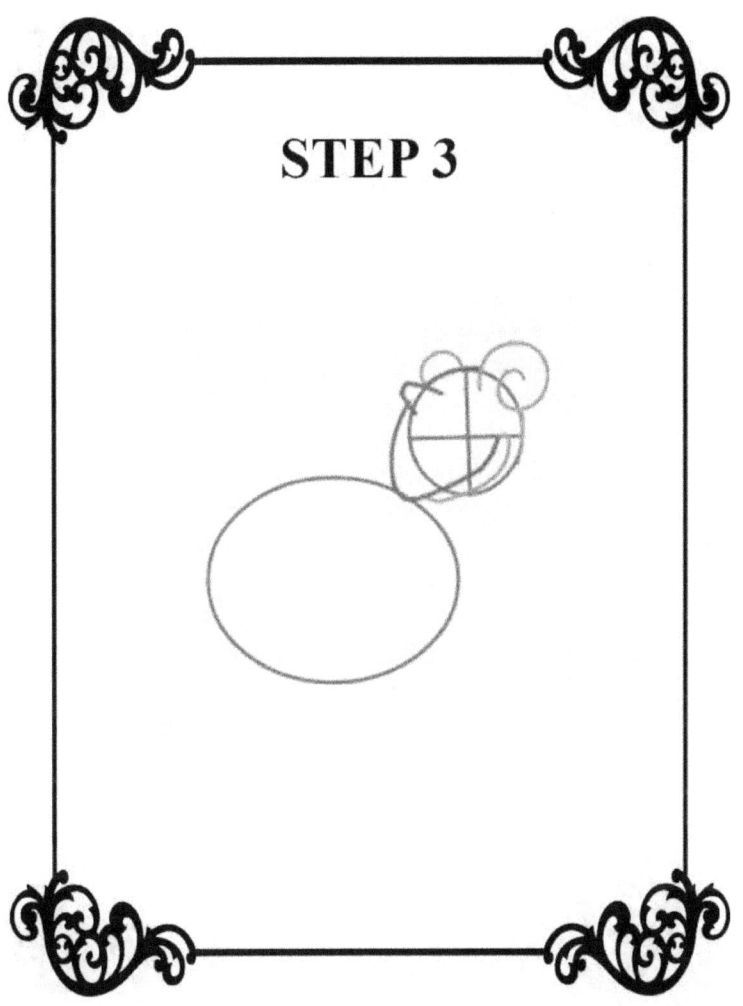

STEP 4

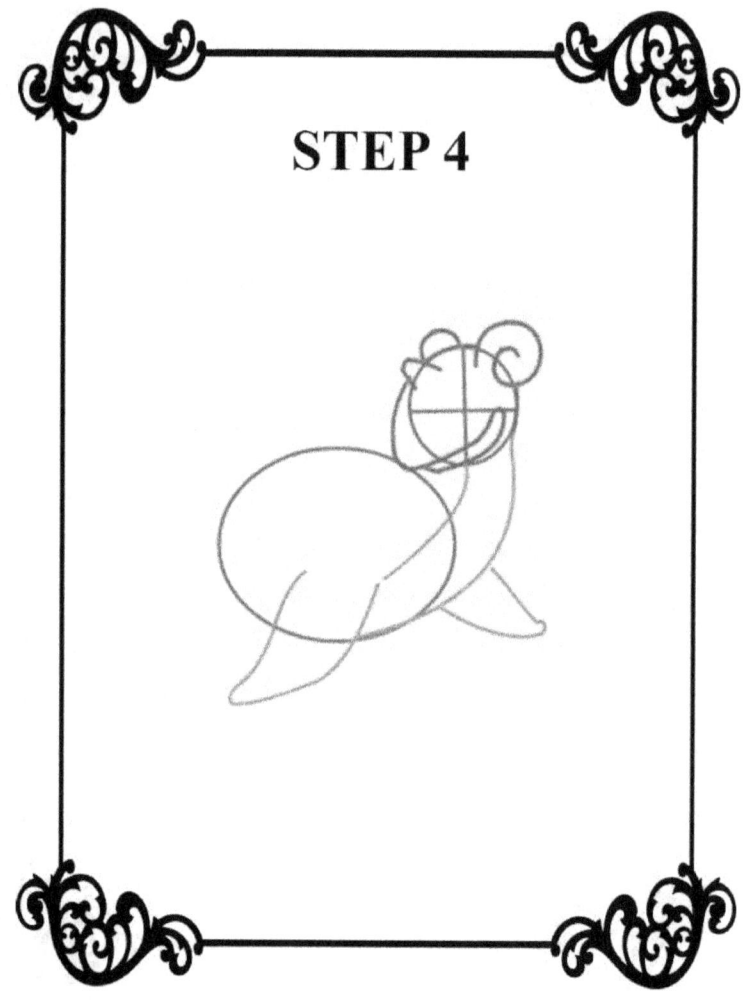

STEP 5

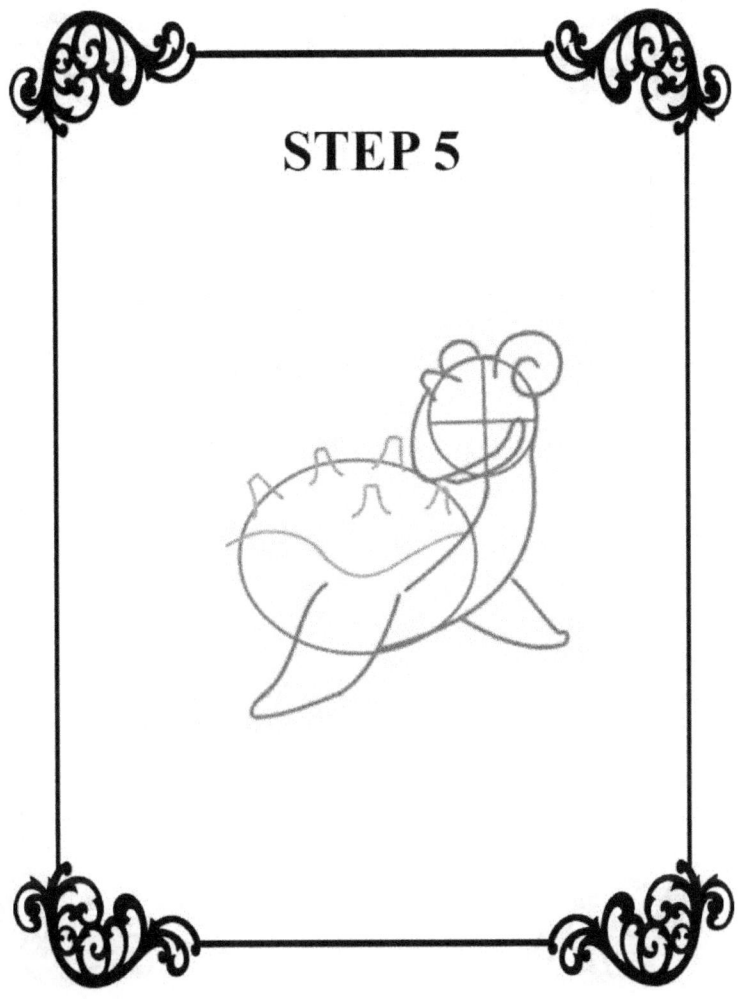

STEP 6

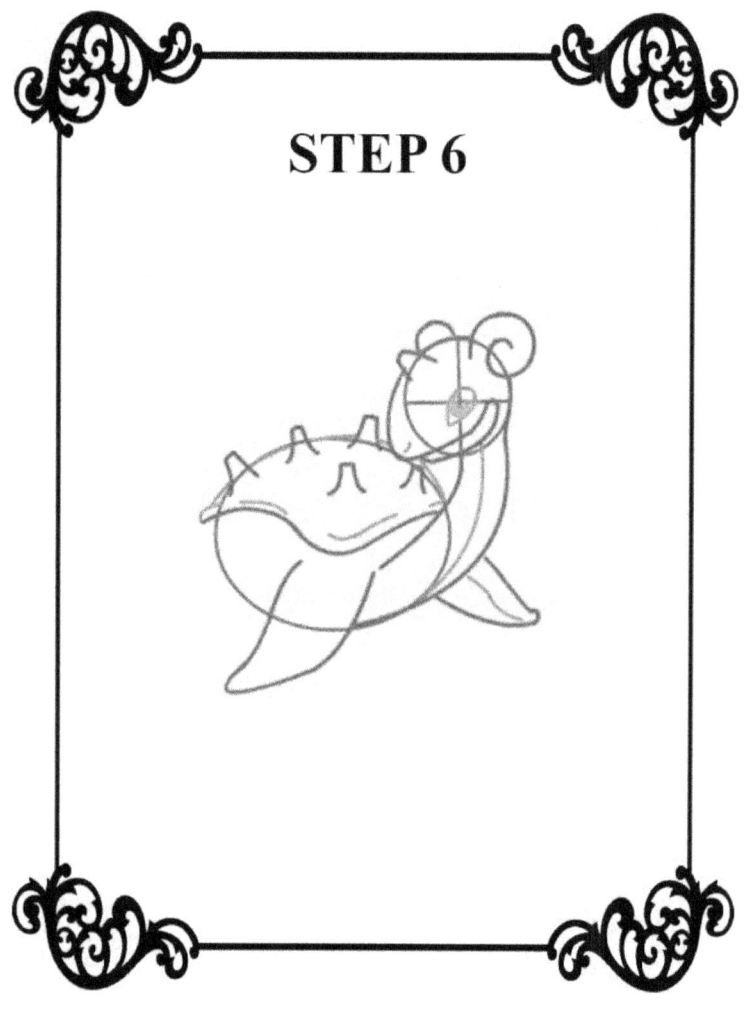

STEP 7

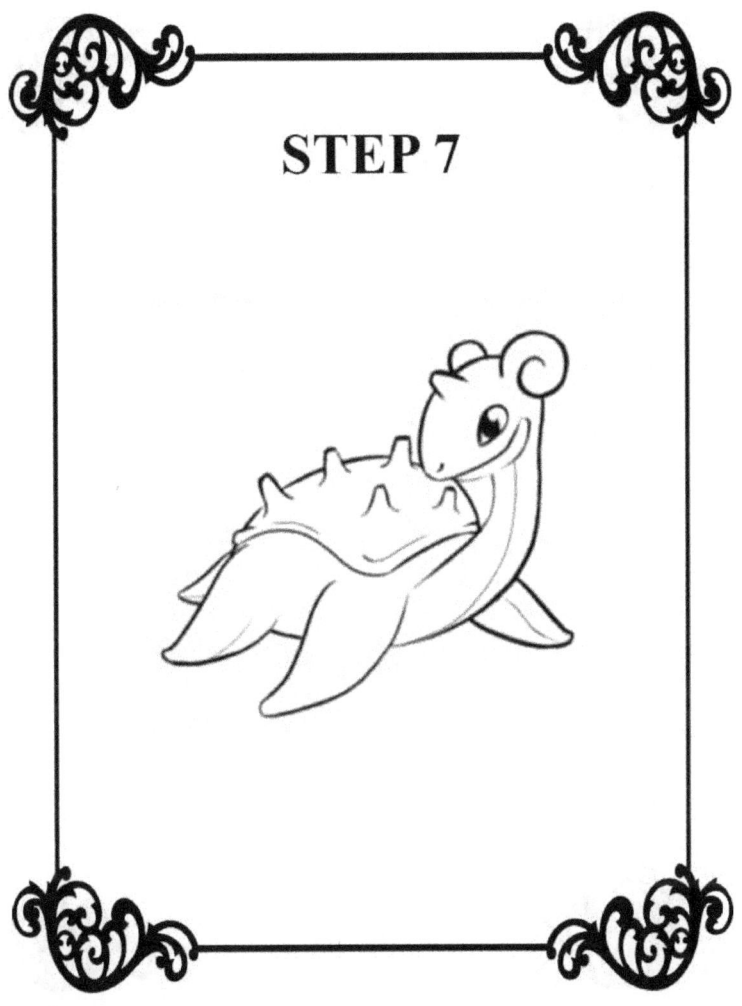

TURTWIG

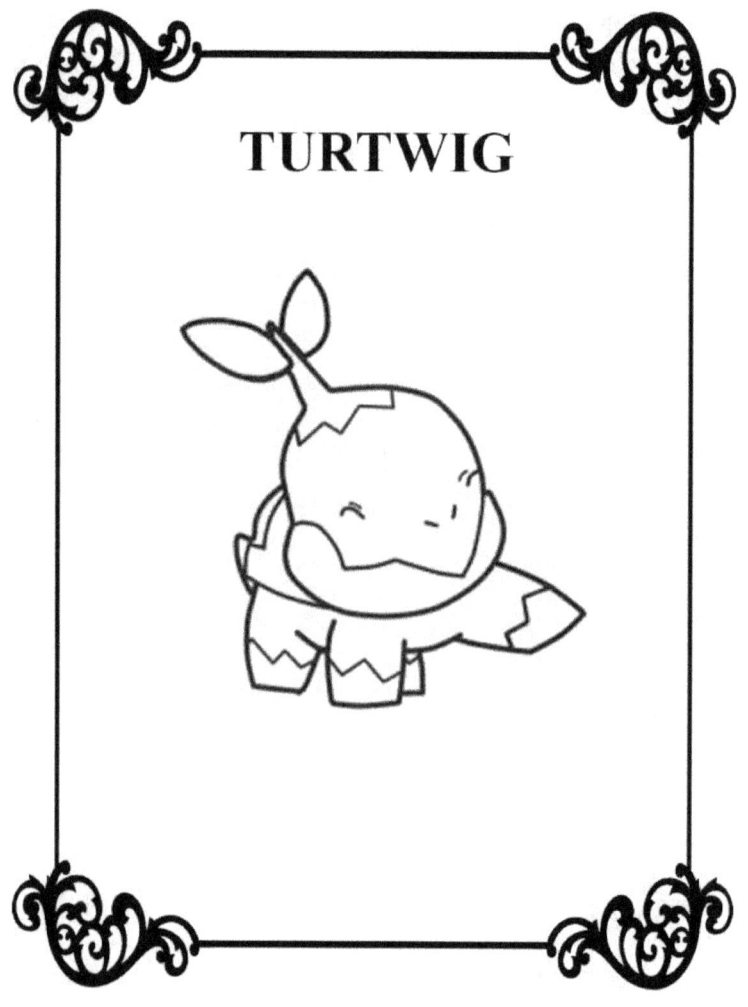

STEP 1

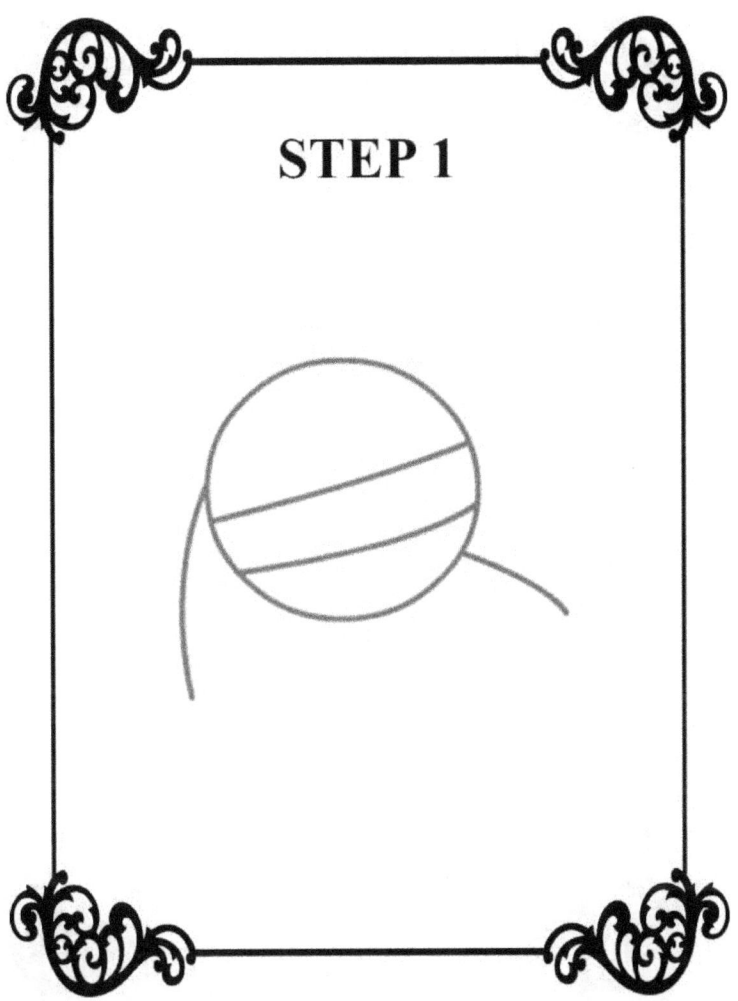

STEP 2

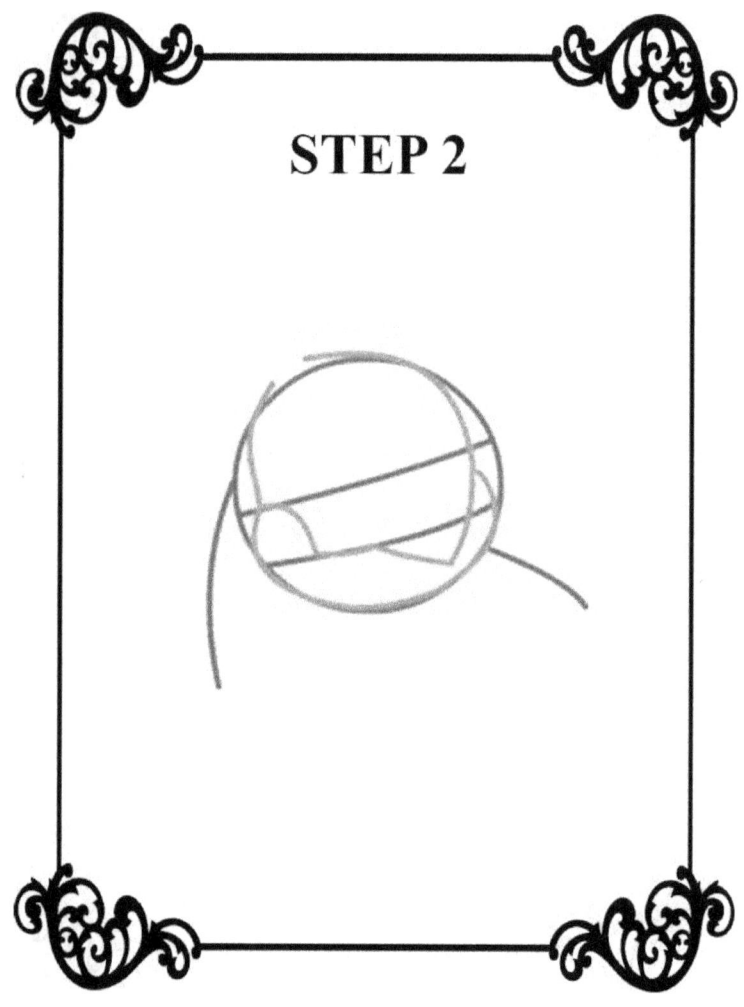

STEP 3

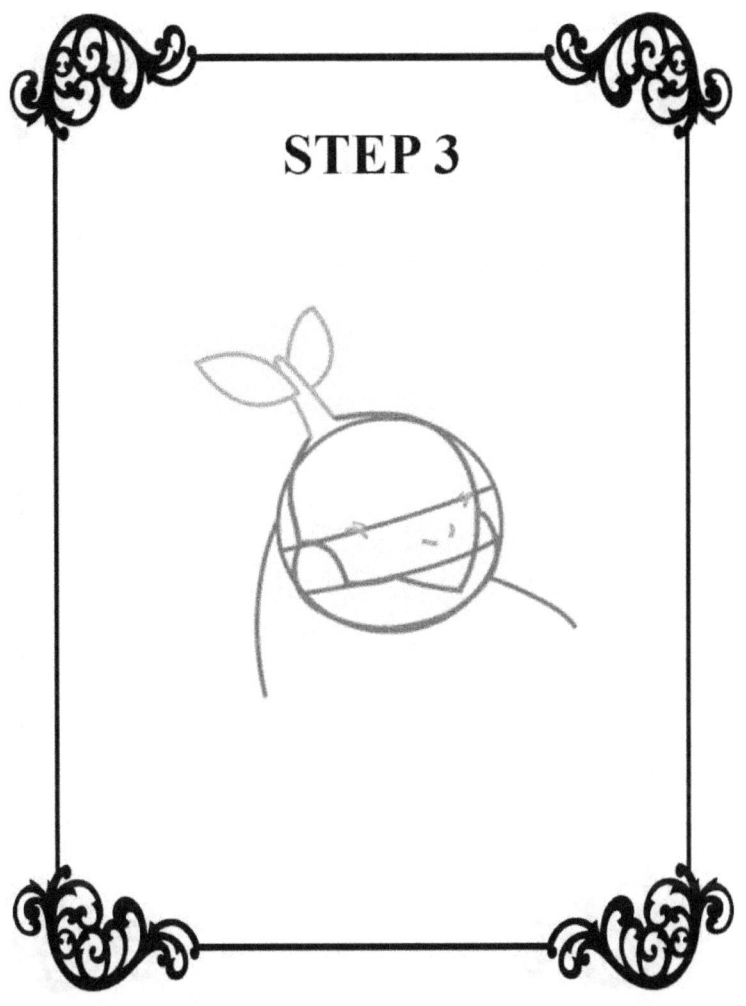

STEP 4

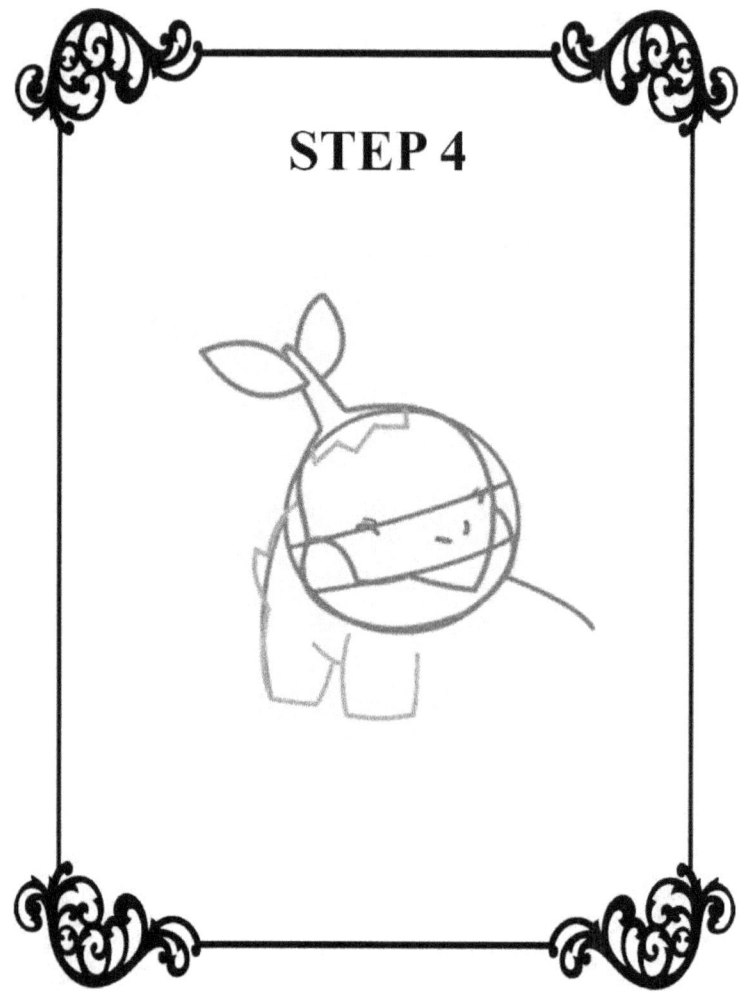

STEP 5

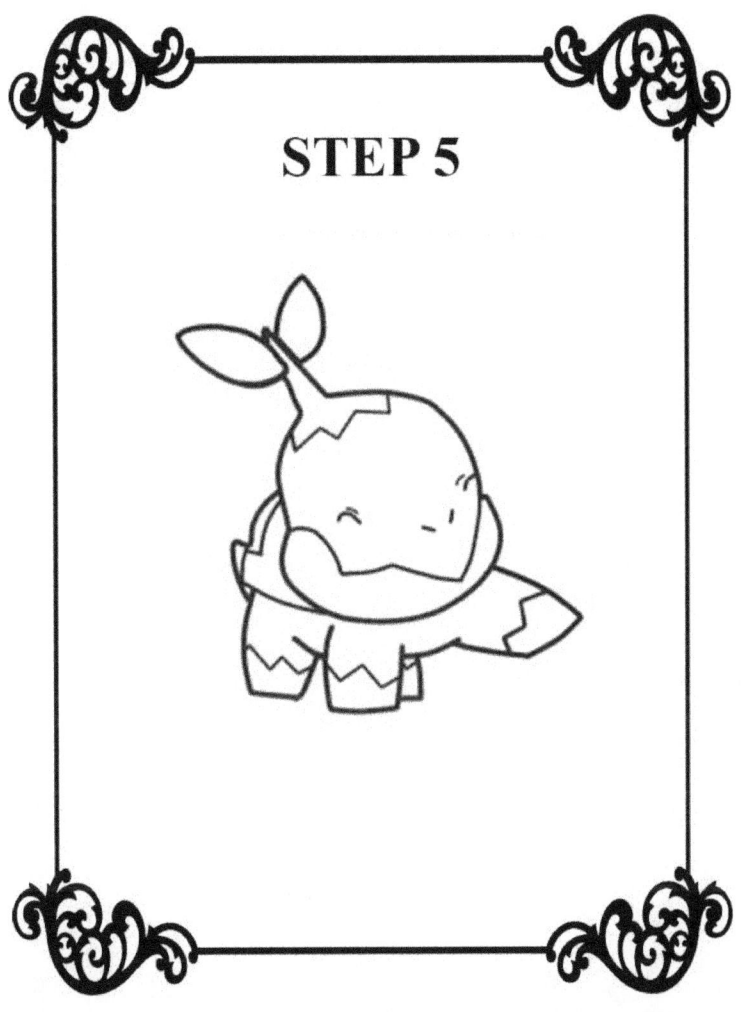